Alexander the Great

A Three-Act Play

To watch the play, please scan the following QR Code:
Alexander the Great

Dr. Sultan bin Muhammad Al-Qasimi

Alexander the Great

A Three-Act Play

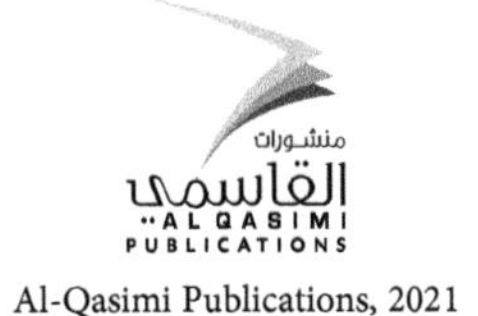

Al-Qasimi Publications, 2021

Alexander the Great - A Three-Act Play
First published in 2006 in Arabic as "Al-Iskandar Al-Akbar"
by: Al-Qasimi Publications
Author: Dr. Sultan bin Muhammad Al-Qasimi (United Arab Emirates)
Publisher Name: Al-Qasimi Publications
Sharjah, United Arab Emirates
Edition: First
Year of publication: 2021

Translated from the Arabic by: Dr. Ahmed Ali

ISBN: 978-9948-469-55-1
Printing Permission: National Media Council, Abu Dhabi, UAE
No. MC 01-03-5083265, Date: 05-08-2021

Age Classification: E
The age group that matches the content of the books was classified according to the age classification issued by the National Council for Media
----
Al- Qasimi Publications, Al Tarfa, Sheikh Mohammed Bin Zayed Road
PO Box 64009 Sharjah, United Arab Emirates
Tel: 0097165090000, Fax: 0097165520070
Email: info@aqp.ae

Cover Image: Alexander the Great in mosaic,
House of the Faun, Pompei, Italy.

CONTENTS

Foreword

This play is inspired by the many major works of history on Alexander the Great. It depicts a living image of the power struggle in the past and present and wherever it takes place.

The events of this play are well researched and properly documented as per the Reference List at the end.

-The Author-

Cast of Characters

According to appearance

- Council of Alexander
- Hajib
- Alexander
- A Councilor
- Commanders
- Advisors
- Persian Envoy
- Parmenion
- Darius's envoys and ambassadors
- Intelligence Agent
- Amýntas
- A group of soldiers and guards

- Polemon
- Polydamas
- Two Arabs
- A Commander
- Ptolemy
- Two soldiers
- Polydamas
- Bessus
- Two men in Arab attire
- Cleitus
- Phegeus
- Coenus
- A soldier
- Porus
- Nearchus
- A group of sailors
- Carriage Driver
- Locals (Babylonians)
- A group of Western ambassadors
- Explorer Commanders

Act One

Scene I

Place: Gaugamela, south east Mosul, after a battle when Darius, King of Persia, was defeated, his mother, wife and children captured.

Time: October, 331 BCE

Setting: Large tent of Alexander's. His Council members are sitting, each talking to the person sitting next to him.

(The Hajib enters.)

Hajib *(annopuncing)*: Alexander, the Great.

(The Council is silent and the members stand up in respect for Alexander.

Alexander enters walking proudly. He greets the Council and points to the members to sit. He sits at the head of the meeting table facing the audience).

Alexander: How are our brave fighters?

Council: We're fully-prepared for the next battle.

Alexander: An envoy from Drius, King of Persia, has arrived.

A Councilor: Another envoy? He has already sent ten envoys with two peace proposals. And you, my Lord, have rejected them.

Alexander: Let's hear what he has to say this time. The envoy is a relative of King Darius.

(Alexander claps his hands and the Hajib enters.)

Alexander: Allow the Persin envoy in.

(Alexander to his Commanders):

Alexander: No peace with these people. Before you know it, their authority had extend to Sidon and Tire where they strtted to build ships. What were they after? We have manged to destroy them at those ports and will not stop pursuing them until we get to their borders with India.

(The Hajib calls):

Hajib: Envoy of Persia.

(The Persian envoy enters, dressed in a Princely attire. He bows down a few times greeting Alexander).

(A moment of silence)..

(Alexander to the Persian envoy):

Alexander: Speak.

Persian Envoy: King Darius is sad for the death of his wife. He is requesting from you the release of his elderly mother and his two married daughters in return for 180 million Drachmas. He is also proposing that you marry his eldest daughter. He is requesting peace. In return, he will relinquish all the territories west of the Euphrates. He is also prepared to leave his son, Ochus, as a guarantee for the peace process.

Alexander: Anything else?

Persian Envoy: That's all, your Majesty.

(Alexander to the Persian Envoy):

Alexander: You may leave and wait in the Guest tent.

(Alexander claps and the Hajib enters. Alexander waves the Persian envoy to be escorted to the Guest Tent).

(Alexander to his Council):

Alexander: What say you about Darius's proposal?

(No response from the Council. Alexnader walks about in the tent waiting for a response. The Council members look at one another, but no one dares express his opinion, as they do not know what Alexander's view is on the matter. They cannot have a view contradictory to his. Eventually Parmenion picks up some courage and responds after Alexander solicits his opinion)

Alexander: What do you think, Parmenion?

(Parmenion advances towards Alexander and speaks with an arrogant tone):

Parmenion: You all know my opinion; that is, you release the prisoners from Damascus in return for a ransom. You will receive a large sum. Guarding those prisoners has occupied the time of many of our soldiers. Now, you will be able to collect 180 M

Drachmas just to release and old woman and two girls. In fact, their presence is obstructing the advance of our troops. It is possible to creat a wealthy kingdom through neotiations instead of wars. What benefit is there from all the land we have occupied from Phonicia to the Euphrates? Your Majesty, these are mere expanses of desert that no one has ever been able to control before you. I advise that you return to Macedonia and cease the advance to India.

(Alexander looks angry at what Parmenion said and the way he spoke).

Alexander: Yes. I would also prefer money to military glory ... if I were Parmenion! But, I am Alexander. I do not care for riches. I am a King, not a merchant. I have no goods to sell. If I want to release someone, I do it by way of a favour from me; not for the sake of a payment.

(Alexander claps and the Hajib enters. Alexander instructs him):

Alexander: Bring the Persian envoy back.

(A while later the Persian envoy enters).

(Alexander to the Persian envoy):

Alexander: Inform Draius that I have no desire for peace. The territories we conquered, rather all the territories under his rule will soon be spoils of war in the hands of my army. The borders between our empires will be dictated by war shortly.

Persian Envoy: Since Alexander is bent on war, may you allow me to leave to inform King Darius of such in order that the matter is not a hoax.

(Alexander claps and the Hajib enters. Alexander instructs him):

Alexander: The Persian envoy may be allowed to leave immediately, together with the other ambassadors and envoys of Darius' that we have kept.

(The Persian envoy exits with the Hajib)

Alexander: He say 'hoax'! This peace proposal is the real hoax.

(The Hajib enters and says):

Hajib: My Lord! The Intelligence officer is at your door.

Alexander: Let him in.

(The Intelligence officer enters).

Intelligence Officer: My Lord! We have received information that Darius has deployed 3000 cavalrymen under the commandship of Manos; and they are advancing towards us.

Alexander: Did I not say 'it was all a hoax'. Commanders, let each of you go to his battalion and prepare for the fight against our enemy.

-Blackout-

Scene II

Place: Herat, on the way to Kandahar.

Setting: Alexander's large tent with a gathering of commanders and advisors.

(Alexander walks into the tent looking furious):

Alexander: A consoiracy? Against my life? And by whom? My own commanders? The nearest people to me?

(Alexander shouts):

Alexander: Amýntas. Your brother is among them?!

(Amýntas rushes to kneel at the feet of Alexander and says):

Amýntas: My brother, Polemon is innocent of this conspiracy. I seek your forgiveness, my Lod. Please, forgive him. I beg you.

(A group of soldiers enters with their swords up. Between them is Polemon, chained and dragged on the ground. Polemon shows no signs of fear).

Alexander: You are with them, Polemon?

Polemon: I shall not defend myself .. if my escape is to cause harm to my brother..

(He points at Amýntas who is kneeling before Alexnader):

Polemon: When I saw the soldiers chasing Parminion's sone, Philotas, and killing him, I feared for my life and ran away. They caught me and brought me here.

(Polemon bursts into tears and hits his face with his two hands)

Amýntas: What a stupid thing to do! What were running away for? And to whom?

Attendees: Forgive him, my Lord! Grant him your forgiveness!

Alexander: Amýntas, I am aware of your loyalty

to me, and will therefore forgive your brother. I will. Untie him.

(Polemon rushes to kiss Alexander's feet after being freed; but Alexander stops him saying)"

Alexander: Take your brother and go.

(A moment of silence).

Alexander: You may all leave.

(As they are leaving Alexander shouts for one of the commanders):

Alexander: Polydamas, stay a while.

(Polydamas stays alone with Alexander who addresses him):

Alexander: Do you know who the Chief conspirator is? It is your close friend, Parmenion, who stayed behind in Media *(Hamedam)* and did not join our march to India. He is my friend and yours. We both will be his victims. Therefore, I want you to kill him. Go to Media where Parmenion is. Hand this message of mine to the Governor there. He will assist you in making the necessary arrangments to carry out the assassination. To avoid Parmenion doubting your intentions, here is a letter I have written with my own hand, and sealed it with the seal of his son, Philotas. I obtained the seal after he was killed.

(Polydamas shakes his head in fear and hesitation as he takes the letter. Alexander rushes to say):

Alexander: Listen! This is just between you and me. If you divulge my secret or hesitate to carry out my instructions, I am keeping your brother hostage until you return with the good news.

Polydamas: I am at your command, my Lord

(Alexander claps and the Hajib enters).

Alexander: Bring the two Arabs.

(A moment of silence)

(Two Arabs enter; one of them is carrying some clothes).

Alexander: Did you bring the Arabian clothes?

An Arab: Yes, here they are.

(Alexander points to the Arab to hand the clothes to Polydamas).

(Alexander to Polydamas):

Alexander: Go inside and change into your Arabian attire.

(Polydamas exits).

(Silence)

(Alexander to the two Arabs):

Alexander: You will take this man to Media. Be warned that no one knows anything about this trip. If you reveal any information about it or escape, rest assured that your wives and children are hostage here until you return with this man safely.

(Silence).

Alexander: How long is it to Media via the desert?

An Arab: Ten days.

(Polydamas enters dressed in his Arabian attire which he shows Alexander).

(Alexander to the two Arabs):

Alexander: You go get your camels ready and he will catch up with you. Go.

(Silence)

(Alexander to Polydamas)

Alexander: You must hurry so before rumors of the killing of Parmenion's son reach the father's ears. Go on. I want you to bring me Parmenion's head.

(Polydamas exists from one side of the tent. Alexander is about to exit from the other side, but he is stopped by noise outside the tent. He looks out. A commander rushes in shouting):

A Commander: Darius is dead! He has been killed. My Lord. Darius has been killed in the mountains. His officer Bessus killed him.

Alexander: His officer did so while we who were pursuing the king and his commanders were too busy with a conspiracy.

Commander: Your army is now chasing the Persian Commander Bessus who is hiding in the mountain.

Alexander: Well, we must hunt him. He must be captured and brough alive to me here.

-Blackout-

Act Two

Scene I

Place: Marakanada (Samarkand)

Time: 328 BCE

Setting: Alexander's Tent

(A group of commanders chatting. Alexander enters and he is greeted by bowing)

Alexander: Bessus, the Persian commander has declared himself King of Persia. He has taken the name Ardashir Shah upon his coronation. This tenacious man has also dared to attack us. Our troops are chasing him and he will soon be captured.

(Noise outside the tent. One of the commanders, Ptolemy, enters. He is holding a whip in his hand.

Two soldiers follow him dragging the Persian Bessus who is half-naked with wooden ring round his neck. Each soldier holds one side of the neck ring chains.)

Alexander: What are the latest news, Ptolemy?

(Ptolemy points at the Persian commander as he enters).

Ptolemy: Bessus! The Persian commander.

Alexander examines the Persian commander with his eyes.

Alexander: Bessus! At last, you are in my hands. Why did you kill Darius? Wasn't he your king who honoured you and showered you with his kindness? You kill him to take his place as king?!

Bessus: It was not me who killed him; a group of my followers did.

Alexander: With you dead, Bessus, the Persian resistance will end, and we'll get some rest.

Bessus: No, you won't, Your Highness. My successor and ally, Spitamenes, is advancing towards you. The resistance has started everywhere.

Alexander: Ptolemy, kill him.

Ptolemy: No, Your Majesty. Not here. We will cut off his nose and ears, and put him in display in the most populated town in Persia first. Then we execute him.

Alexander: Take him out.

(Ptolemy shouts at Bessus).

Ptolemy: Come on.

(He whips the ground near Bessus's feet and shouts):

Ptolemy: Move.

(A commander to Alexander):

Commander: My Lord, if what Bessus says is true that the resistance has begun, and considering that in yesterday's battle we lost 2000 of our soldiers, this means we only have 35,000 soldiers left. We are so far away from home, and ...

Alexander: That's not a problem, not at all. There are large troops arriving soon from the west.

(A moment of silence).

(Alexander walks about in the tent, thinking about the Persian resistance. A man dressed in an Arabin

attire and looking exhausted walks in. He is holding the head of a man. Two men in Arabian attire follw him. Alexander looks at them).

Alexander: Who is this? Polydamas?

(Polydamas nods that it is him).

Alexander: What is it you're holding in your hands?

Polydamas: This .. is Parminion's head, as you, my Lord, had commanded.

(Cleitus, an old commander, and one of Parminion's friends screams in shock):

Cleitus: What? What is this? What is this?

The other commanders hold him back. One of them tries to calm him down):

A Commander: Cleitus, just sit down. Sit.

(Alexander throws Cleitus an apple from a fruit tray placed on a table).

Alexander: Take him out of here.

(Two commanders take Cleitus out of the tent. Then they return to their places. Polydamas exits with the two Arabs from the other side of the tent).

(Silence)

(Alexander addresses the commanders with his back to the entrance of the tent. Through the entrance Cleitus looks at Alexander and listens very tensely to what he says):

Alexander: Parminion was the Chief conspirator. They have spread rumors among the soldiers that Parminion was the maker of our victories. When he stayed behind the army, who made these victories? It was I. I, Alexander the Great. The son of god Amon. I am not King Philip's son. Even the victories of King Philip were made by me ... not by the Macedonians.

(Cleitus rushes into the middle of the tent and addresses Alexander):

Cleitus: You call yourself the son of a god, while telling lies to these young commanders?! When you turned your back to the battlefield, it was the blood of the Macedonians and their injuries that made you great. And now, you deny your own father and claim to be the son of god Amon?!

Alexander, furious, screams at Cleitus):

Alexander: You, scum of the earth! You think I will let you talk about me like this?

Cleitus: You call me 'scum of the earth', you ingrate. Wasn't it I who taught you how to shoot? Wasn't it my sister who raised you as a child?!

(A group of commanders take Cleitus away from Alexander, but he manages to free himself from them and continues to reproach Alexander):

Cleitus: You have killed my friend Parminion after all the victories he made for you, nd after he had given two of hs own sons defending you! Then you are going to kill their third brother ... in their honour?!

(Alexander searches for his dagger, which he had left on the table behind him. A guard had picked and hidden it in order that Alexandes may not use it to kill Cleitus.

Cleitus heads for the tent entrance, but Alexander snatches a spear from one of the guards and rushes towards Cleitus who is now near the entrance. Alexander throws the spear at Cleitus's chest. The force of the throw pushes Cleitus agaist the entrance curtain. Cleitus screams in pain and falls to the ground with the spear deep in his chest).

(Silence)

Alexander turns to his commanders. His anger subsided. He looks at the commanders who have their mouths open in shock and fear. Alexander himself is astonished as to the turn of events).

(Silence)

(Alexander rushes to Cleitus's body and removes the bloody spear, which he then directs to his own throat.

The commanders rush to hold Alexander, but he walks to the wall of the tent with the spear directed to his chest. They hold him again and remove the spear off his hands. Alexander falls on the ground in exhaustion. He cries):

Alexander: O, Lanice! My dear nanny! I killed your brother. Your sons were killed defending me! How did I retun your favours on me? You raised me as a child and I now kill your brother with my own hands! Oh! Oh! I am a murderer, a murderer! I am the murderer of his own friends! I am the murderer of his own friends!

(The commanders hold Alexander and assist him as he exits the stage).

-Blackout-

Scene II

Place: open ground with two commanders there.

(Commander Phegeus and Commander Coenus.

Coenus sits on a tree stump thinking. On one side of the stage, Alexander's tent entrance is showing. On the other side of the stage is Commander Phegeus.

Coenus calls):

Coenus: Commander Phegeus!

(Commander Phegeus turns to where the sound is coming from).

Phegeus: Who is it? Commander Coenus?

Coenus: Yes. What is the news?

Phegeus: For two days now, I have been trying to persuade him not to cross the river to fight Porus, the Indian Prince. Today, he's decided to cross over!

Coenus: Why? We have reached the end of the Persian Empire Borders. This should be the end of the war.

Phegeus: Alexander says he has divine orders … from Amon who's promised him that he would conquer the whole world.

(Alexander walks out of his tent. The two commanders greet him)

Alexander: Phegeus, I asked you for more information about the Indian Prince Porus. Have you got any yet?

Phegeus: What Porus had said about the power of his tribe is true. No exaggeration of any kind. Their prince is not only a man from among the people, but from a lower class, too. His father was a barber who made his living through hard work. It was owing to his good looks that the Princess introduced him to the ruling Prince. He became very close to him and that is how he killed the Prince and seized the kingdom. He then took the Princess as a wife and got rid of the children of the former Prince.

Alexander: I am more interested in the war situation.

Phegeus: As you can see, my Lord, we have this wide rocky river ahead of us. Then, there is a barren desert that goes on for twelve days. If we cross all this, we get to the campr area of Prince Porus. The road to there is blocked by 20,000 cavalrymen and 200,000 infantry soldiers backed by 1000 horse carriages; not to mention the 3,000 scary elephants among his troops. This where Prince Porus is camped behind the river.

Coenus: Very large force ... in addition to the other obstacles: the river and desert ...

Alexander: We are not less powerful. We have our local forces and the forces coming from Greece. Our army will reach 200,000 men.

(Silence).

Alexander (calling):

Alexander: Coenus, gether the soldiers. I will speak to them.

(Coenus callas the soldiers).

Coenus: Fellow soldiers! Come forth to listen to the king!

(The soldiers stand in some rows on one side of the stage)

Alexander: My brave men! It has come to my attention that the Indians have been spreading rumours and that has been a source of disturbance for you. Regardless of these rumours, false and fabricated reports should not worry you in the least. You used to fught small forces. Now, for the first time, you will be facing a rogue tribe. I seek your assistance in your courageous hearts and strong arms. These are what will secure our victory and get us to reach our goal. The rewards are greater than the risks. These lands are rich, but not well-versed in the art of war. Today, I do not lead you to gory, but to the booty and spoils of war. You deserve to possess that wealth which the sea has thrown at the shores of India and take it to your homeland. Let me say that I am not addressing you today as your king, rather I am your leader who has successfully taken you to the end of the earth. Previously. I made commands; but this time I will owe you this. I ask you to persevere as I share with you the risks we have taken and will protect you with my shield.

(Some moments of silence).

Alexander: Why are you silent? Where are your aspirational shouts? Where are your Macedonian looks that are hungry for glory? My men! It seems as if I no longer know you or you me!

(As Alexander talks, his men keep silent with their heads down)

Alexander: Perhaps, I inadvertently wronged you to the point that you no longer want to look at me. Is that true? No one is to answer me? No one says, no. Whom am I addressing then? What is it that I asked for? It is your glory. It is your greatmess that I work for and seek to realize. Where are those men who yesterday vied with one another to carry their injured king? Well, I shall desert you and abandon my responsibilities as your leader. I shall give up myself to my enemies whom I had fought against, the Persians. They will be my men .. Death is better than being a leader who follows the whims of others. Well, return to to your homeland. Desert your king. Take your victory with you. I am able to bring that victory, which you despaired of realizing. If I cannot, I will die with dignity!

(Nothing Alexander says has any effect on the men who continue to be silent. They were counting on their commanders to speak up for then and tell Alexander they were exhausted and injured. However, the commanders also had their heads down in fear of Alexander.

All of a sudden, some grumbling voice are heard, followed by sounds of pain. The men start to voice their concerns. Some cry and burst into tears. Alexander is even moved to tears himself by this and his anger turns to sympathy. Everyone present is now in tears.

Coenus picks up some courage and approaches Alexander while the rest of the commanders stand where they are. He takes off his helmet and seeks permission to speak. The other commanders encourage him to speak about the state of the army).

A man: Coenus, speak for us. talk about the problems we are facing in the army.

Coenus: May God keep all evil intentions away from us. This is how we trust our soldiers. Your men are ready as they have always been to go with you wherever you take them: to war, to danger, to death. We will fight to raise your name high... We are ready to go anywhere you please. We will serve in your ranks with or without arms. We will serve naked and exhausted. But, could you just hear a few sincere words from your devout soldiers? You are currently in a different world and are about to enter yet another new one. You are going to expose this trained army to wild animals. I want you to hear this from me and not from the soldiers behind you … our arms are broken, wounds bleeding and we have no horses to ride …

(The men start to raise their voices and shout):

Soldiers: Alexander is our King! Alexander, our patron. Alexander, our Lord!

(Silence)

(Alexander could not put any blame on his men, but he is not free from anger. He looks confused. He calls for his entourage to follow him to his tent).

Alexander: Only my entourage is to follow me.

Phegeus follows Alexander, then he returns to say to everyone):

Phegeus: You may all leave. Get ready to cross the river.

(Quiet)

(After a short while, Alexander comes out of his tent holding a book. He sits on a tree stump and starts to read. He notices Ptolemy looking at the entrance of his tent):

Alexander: Ptolemy, Ptolemy! Approach.

(Ptolemy walks towards Alexander).

Alexander: Shortly, we will start to cross the river.

(Ptolemy looks at the book next to Alexander on the tree stump. He picks it up and reads the title):

Ptolemy: 'The Book of India' by Tesias. You really cannot wait, right?

Alexander: No, I cannot. When we have conquered India, we could only then say that the whole of Asia is in our hands. Afterwards, we will return home. We will start to change the world, Ptolemy.

Ptolemy: Do you think the world can be changed? You think we can succeed in this project?!

Alexander: I believe we can. You remember when we were young how we used to dream and how we were full of ambition and hope?! Those little children have now defeated the greatest empire on the face of the earth .. that is, one third of the world. We built the Greek cities and established Greek laws at the heart of Asia. Do you think all those wars were pointless?

Ptolemy: No, not at all. There has to be an objective for those wars.

(Silence)

(Phegeus enters and addresses Alexander):

Phegeus: My Lord! We have started to cross the river.

Alexander: Is it dawn time now?

Phegeus: Just about, my Lord!

(Alexander goes to his tent to wear his military gear).

(Lights are dimmed).

(The soldiers are heard chanting war songs. Then sounds of battle fighting ensue).

-Blackout-

Scene III

Place: Battlefield

Setting: The stage is lit where Alexander is leaning on a tree. The marks of fighting are seen on him. He has taken off his helmet and placed his sword and shield beside him. He stands with some of his commanders.

Alexander: How long were we in battle?

A Commander: Eight hours.

Alexander: We defeated Porus. He was not just a leader, but a brave fighter, too. I have sent him his friend, Meroes, to bring him in order for us to have a peace treaty with him.

(A commander arrives)

The Commander: Porus is on his way here.

(Alexander wears his helmet).

Meroes entrs with Porus who is tall, handsome with wide shoulders. He is wounded on his right shoulder.

(Alexander addresses Porus):

Alexander: How would you like me to treat you?

Porus: You treat me the way you should treat a Prince.

(Alexander pleased with Porus's answer):

Alexander: For me, this should be fine. But is there something else you desire?

Porus: Everything is in my initial request.

(Alexander looks even happier)

Alexander: We have returned to you all the territories we occupied, kept you as a Prince ruling your country and made you a friend of ours providing that you fight with us in our future battles.

Porus: You have got my word.

(Porus exits)

(Alexander talks to his commanders)

Alexander: Now, we need to return to Persia and stay in Babylon.

-Blackout-

Act Three

Scene I

Place: The Persian Coast near the entrance to the Gulf.

Setting: A few miles away from the coast. Alexander meets with Nearchus who is coming from India by sea. Alexander had sent him to explore India.

(Alexander enters from one side of the stage followed by rejoicing soldiers. Nearchus enters from the other side followed by rejoicing sailors.

As soon as Alexander approaches Nearchus, they both run to hug each other. They embrace and look at each other in disbelief. They could hardly speak. Eventually, Alexander laughs loudly and says while standing back):

Alexander: Nearchus! You smell like rotten fish!

Bearchus: And you smell of sweaty horses.

(Alexander looks again at the thin face of his navy officer):

Alexander: I cannot believe you are still alive.

Neachus: It was not an easy mission. A few times, I even thought I would not be able to complete it. We suffered two storms, but the biggest problem was thirst and hunger.

(Alexander walks around in the camp with Nearchus. They exit from one side of the stage and enter from the other side. Ptolemy stands the soldiers in line to greet him. As they pass, Ptolemy shouts):

Ptolemy: Alalalai![1] King Alexander!

The soldiers raise their spears high and shout loudly):

Soldiers: Alalalai! Alalalai! Alalalai!

Ptolemy: Alalalai! Navy Commander Nearchus!

The soldiers raise their spears high and shout loudly):

Soldiers: Alalalai! Alalalai! Alalalai!

Nearchus: My Lord! We do not have good food

1- Alalalai is a battle cry of the ancient Greek.

except for a little bit of fish that we caught today.

Alexander: This is quite alright. We have a surprise ourselves, and I think it should arrive tomorrow.

Nearchus: I do not think we could wait for your tomorrow's surprise. We are starving. Oh! If I tell you what hunger had done to us! We were attacking some coastal villages… could you tell what we looted?!

Alexander: No, I do not know, but I think .. it was …

Nearchus: Fish. Yes, bags and bags of fish. Those miserable poor had nothing but fish.

A Sailor: Gentlemen, the grilled fish is ready.

(Alexander and the commanders walk to one side of the stage while joking and laughing. Suddenly, battle drums are heard. Alexander shouts):

Alexander: O, Zeus!Who on earth is he who dares attack us now?!

(Alexander pulls out his sword, and shouts):

Alexander: Commanders, mount your horses. Mount your horses.

(The sounds of battle drums and horses are all over the camp. The palm-branch fence falls as the soldiers are rushing and pushing one another. Behind the fallen fence dust is stirred and then soldiers surrounding a horse-carriage are seen).

(Silence) ..

The horse-carriage appears on the stage. It can be seen clearly after the dust dissipates. A group of soldiers holding their swords and wearing the shields surround it. A man gets off the horse-carriage. He looks exhausted from travelling. His face is almost covered with dust. He holds some food and drink, and shouts):

Carriage Driver: We have brought you wine and plenty of food.

(Alexander, the commanders and soldiers laugh hysterically).

Alexander and the commanders sit on the ground.

Nearchus arrives with a map, which he open before them all):

Nearchus: This is a map drawn on a papyrus paper. We have drawn on it our trip from India to here. At the moment, we are here, my Lord.

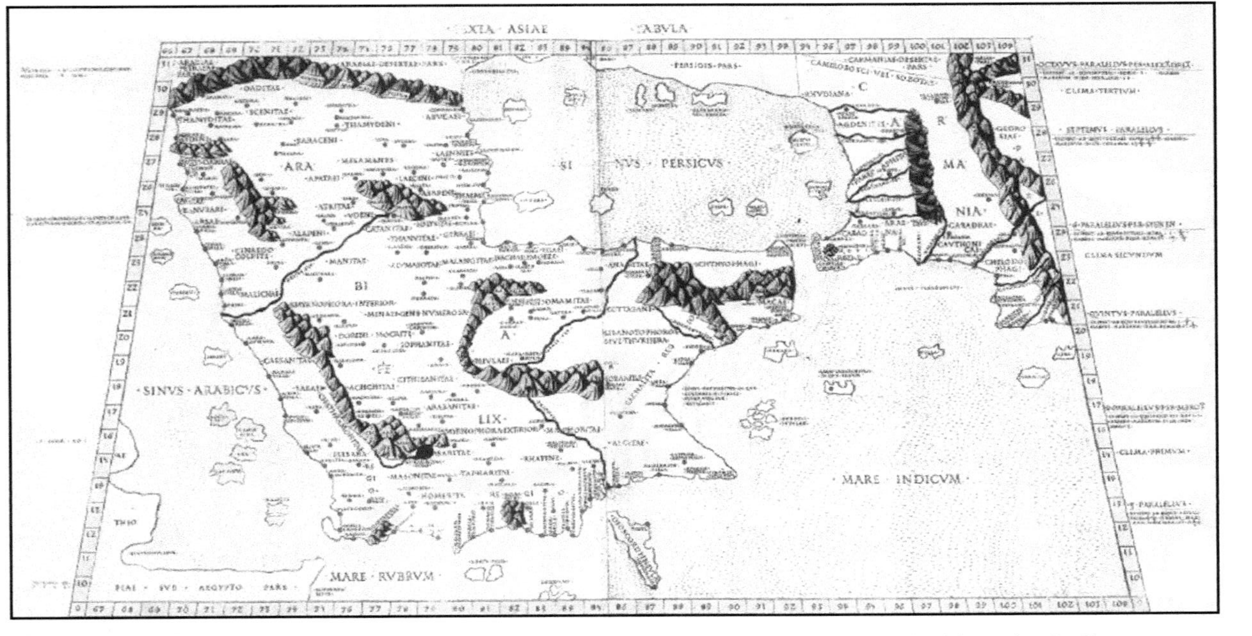

The Fish Eaters' Arena (currently the UAE). A reproduction of the original map seen by Alexander the Great.

(Alexander moves his finger on the map and says):

Alexander: Great. But what is this coast overlooking the Gulf?

(Alexander tries to read something on the map):

Alexander: Fish Eaters! Fish Eaters!

Nearchus: This has been written by the navy Vice-Commander.

Alexander: Why did you name it so?

Nearchus: All they have is fish! Even their sheep smell like fish.

(Alexander asks):

Alexander: Are they Arabs?

Nearchus: Yes. This is the eastern side of the Arabian Peninsula.

(Alexander to Nearchus):

Alexander: Those Arabs have never sent us an ambassador, and never declared they were our vassals. They have become the only ones in the region who have not been subjugated to my rule. All other nations offered me their loyalty and obedience except for them. Therefore, the Arabian Peninsula must be conquered. Permanent settlements must be established there. I commission you to make the necessary preparations and discover the roads leading to there.. We meet in Babylon.

-Blackout-

Scene II

Place: Centre of the City of Babylon on the Euphrates river, east of Baghdad. We hear a noise approaching gradually.

Setting: Before Alexander enters the stage ..

(Some local Babylonians rush to meet Alexander who arrives from the other side of the stage. They shout and turn round.

The Locals: Alexander! Alexander!

(Alexander enters the stage walking proudly, looking right and left. He raises his head up and looks at the walls and pillars of the city of Babylon. Behind him are Nearchus and some commanders..

Alexander shouts):

Alexander: Nearchus! Nearchus!

(Nearchus advances to walk next to Alexander while he bows humbly. He says):

Nearchus: I am here, my Lord.

Alexander: Where is your friend, the astrologer, who predicted my death as I enter Babylon? Here I am at the heart of the city. When we crossed the Tigris River, that astrologer spoke to me privately and begged me not to enter Babylon. When I asked him 'why?', he answered there I would meet my destiny. What did he mean by that? What?

Nearchus: He had told me the same, my Lord! But I dared not speak to you about that. I proposed to him that he did that himself. The same goes for the priests. They were all warning against going to Bablyon.

(At this moment, a murder of crows flies above and their cries are heard):

Alexander: What are these cries?

Nearchus: These are the caws of crows.

(A crow falls dead near the feet of Alexander)

Alexander: What is this?

Nearchus: A dead crow. This is a bad omen!

(Alexander to Nearchus):

Alexander: forget this nonsence, and tell me ....

(A man enters holding a letter, which he gives to Alexander. Alexander reads it and looks concerned).

Nearchus: What's wrong, my Lord?

Alexander: This letter confirms that 6,000 of our troops have fled with the money and that they are on their way to Athens as we speak. Bring in the two men who had informed me of the soldiers' fleeing a few days ago.

(A group of soldiers bring in two men in shackles.

Alexander reproaches the soldiers):

Alexander: Removes their chains and shackles. Untie them.

(The soldiers hurry up to remove the chains. Alexander addressing the two men):

Alexander: At first, I did not believe you, and

therefore you were cuffed and shackled. I was wrong. Give them a reward.

(The two men are taken out. Alexander turns to Nearchus):

Alexander: How did you act upon the instructions I gave you at the Gulf entrance?

Nearchus: All is ready, my Lord! The explorers are with me. When you have a spare moment, you may instruct that we present you with the discoveries and plans.

Alexander: Well, in this case, let us celebrate my victories in India, here in the middle of Babylon. Let's go.

-Blackout-

Scene III

Place: Heart of Babylon.

Setting: Celebrations of the victories of Alexander the Great. Present are some western ambassadors. In the middle of the stage to the back is a bug seat for Alexander.

(Alexander enters with Nearchus and the explorer commanders. Alexander heads for his seat and sits on it. Then, he welcomes the western ambassadors):

Alexander: Western Ambassadors, welcome to Babylon. I would like to thank you for joining our celebtations of the great victories we have made. I had commissioned Nearchus to make all the preparations and arrangements for a coming campaign. Here are Nearchus and the explorer commanders to explain to us all those plans. I would like that you hear them from Nearchus.

(Alexander calling Nearchus):

Alexander: Nearchus.

Nearchus advances while Alexander starts to drink glasses of alcohol, one after another.

Nearchus: My Lord instructed me to explore the coasts of the Arabian Peninisula. Accordingly, I sent a ship from Egypt to the Red Sea for this purpose. I also sent three other ships to explore the Arabian coast in the Gulf: one commanded by Archias, who reached the islands of Icarus[1] and Tylus.[2] The second ship was under the command of Androsthenes who explored the Arabian coast beyond Tylus, all the way to the entrance of the Gulf. The third ship was commanded by Heiron who went from the Gulf to the ocean to explore the Arabian coast overlooking the ocean. A port has been constructed on the Euphrates in Babylon, and more than 1,000 warships have been

1- Failaka island.
2- Bahrain.

built and are anchored at the port. The phonician sailors have also arrived and ready to receive my Lord's orders.

(Alexander gets up off his seat. He staggers as he has consumed too much alcohol)

Alexander: Starting tomorrow, all the ships are to be manned and sail in the Euphrates River to the Gulf in order to conquer Arabia. You know why we are doing this? Because the Arabs have not sent us an ambassador, nor declared to be our vassals. They have become the only ones in the region who have not been subjugated to my rule. All other nations offered me their loyalty and obedience except for them. Therefore, the Arabian Peninsula must be conquered. Permaent settlements must be established there. Drink with me to the conquest of Arabia.

(Much noise and loud laughs ensue. Suddenly, a much louder voice is heard. Alexander screams in severe pain):

Alexander: Aaah, aaaah, aaaah.

(All becomes quiet. Alexander is turning and twisting in agony. He screams again):

Alexander: Aaah, aaaah, aaaah.

(A group of commanders rush to assist him.

All present are in shock. Alexander continues to scream in pain.

Alexander: Aaah, aaaah, aaaah.

Lights are dimmed gradually with Alexander's screams getting lower and lower.

Alexander: Aaah, aah, ah.

-Blackout-

Scene IV

Place: Palace of Nebuchadnezzar on the bank of the Euphrates.

Time: June 323 BCE

Setting: A bed in the middle of the stage. Alexander is lying in bed and Nearchus is standing by his side.

(A commander enters).

Commander: How is Alexander today, Nearchus?

Nearchus: Since the celebration day, he has been suffering from a fever, which has not lifted. We had to transfer him to the Palace of Nebuchadnezzar on the bank of the Euphrates, away from Babylon in the hope that his health improves. But, alas, it has not. Everyone was warning him against entering Babylon.

(Knocks on the doors and shouting voices are heard).

Voices: Open the door! We want to see Alexander. Open the door.

The doors open and some unarmed commanders enter. Their heads are down. They walk in a line round Alexnader's bed, then exit .. Alexander is heard moaning in pain):

Alexander: Aaah, aaaah, aaaah.

(Alexander continues to moan so loudly a number of times. Then, suddenly his chest rises. His moans stop and he falls on the bed with one hand hanging to the side of the bed. Nearchus screams in shock):

Nearchus: Alexander the Great has died! Alexander the Great has died! Alexander the Great has died!

(From outside, Nearchus voice is echoed and voices of a group of people chanting religious hymns are mixed with the echo):

Voices: Alexander the Great has died! Alexander the Great has died!

-Blackout-

References:

1. Arrian (2nd century CE). 1971. *The Campaigns of Alexander*. Harmonds Worth: Penguin.
2. Bosworth, A.B. 1988. *Conquest and Empire, the Reign of Alexander the Great*. Cambridge: Cambridge University Press.
3. Budge, Wallis EA. 1896. *The Life and Exploits of Alexander the Great*. London: Combridge University Press.
4. Fox, Robin Lane. 1973. *Alexander the Great*. London: Allen Lane.
5. Hogemann, Peter. 1985. *Alexander der Grosse und Arabien Zetemata*. Monographien zur Klassischen Altertum Swissenschaft, Heft 82. C.H. Beck. Munich.

6. Manfredi, Valerio Massimo. 2001. *Alexander, the Ends of the Earth*. London. Pan Macmillan Ltd.
7. Plutarch (first century CE). 1973. *The Age of Alexander*. London: Penguin.
8. Rufus, Quintus Curtius (probably in the first century CE). 1984. *The History of Alexandria*. London: Penguin.
9. Tarn, W.W. 1948. *Alexander the Great*. (2 Volumes). Cambridge: Cambridge University Press.

www.ingramcontent.com/pod-product-compliance
Ingram Content Group UK Ltd.
Pitfield, Milton Keynes, MK11 3LW, UK
UKHW021958190726
13853UKWH00004B/1598

9 789948 469551